David van den Berg

drawings by Mary Leigh Lear

Publisher's Cataloguing-in-Publication Data

van den Berg, David
   Love letters from an arsonist / written by David van den Berg / drawings by
   Mary Leigh Liear
   ISBN: 978-1-953932-17-4

1. Poetry: General 2. Poetry: American - General I. Title II. Author

Library of Congress Control Number: 2022951352

This book is dedicated to my father, the truest man I will ever know.

Epistle I: Salt River Blues

Epistle II: The Midnight Gospel

Epistle III: Pinecone Son

Epistle I:

Salt River Blues

Salt River Blues

cattails rattle on slick grass banks
while bass holes fill with rusty beer cans and long lost hooks
and mudcats sing 'bout mermaids what grow whiskers and choose tobacco
   over princes.

salt river runs backwards all the way north.
you knew it in your bones but lied through your teeth
'cause a man made of mud can't fly too high before
the sun dries him out and he shatters like clay.

catch me waist deep in that black water.
alligators don't bother me none.
they know their kin and besides
they like the music i make with a bullfrog on vocals
and two mosquitos on fiddle
so i'm doin' fine.

i got it on good authority that lungs don't count cigarettes smoked while drunk.

i learned
the back of a woman is the loneliest thing to see
and
her leavin' don't mean nothin' unless you think she was right to do it
so

i'm doin' fine.

i just keep singing those salt river blues.

first the ghost sits on your chest

Listen! I forgot to tell you I drowned the night you burned down the barn. I could see the embers flying on the wind like fireflies, better than the ballet! The sky was red and loud and I was thankful for the water all around that kept the haints away like the peeling blue paint of the porch. Would you tape newspapers to the walls to keep me from finding you? Or would you bottle me up and keep me safe in the closet until night came so I could ride a sinner like a green broke horse? Listen, the catfish are hungry and the frogs stop singing for no one and I'm fearful of dawn so I'll make this fast. If you miss me like I miss you come down to the swamp on new moon next. The water is filled with phosphorescent life and if you look close you can see my footprints flash. And if you miss me like I miss you follow me down to where my bones rest. Don't worry! The water only hurts at first but soon it's like the womb. And if you miss me like I miss you then when next we speak it won't be through dreams but I will be in a body, mine, and you will be in yours, and we will spend our nights as ghosts and never be apart.

now that my arms have become spades

let's now pretend the fallen oranges were ripe
    and you liked the fruit i snuck to the ICU.

the rats have grown large this year,
    their white bellies shake as they run

turning tan in the dry dirt
    beneath the doublewide trailer.

here i will bury three dogs, marked only by a pile of dirt
    that will suffocate the things that try to grow.

here is the day you point to the fourteen plots you bought
    as though i might escape you in death. the idea

troubles you as together we walk the long pavement
    to the torn down house and back twice.

and still the rats feast in the orchard.
    today i will pick unripe citrus

from where they have fallen off greenrot trees
    and taste bitterness come heavy as winter clothes.

i will drive the tomcat from where he has nestled
    between rusted shotguns that still smell

of saltpeter and stale iron.
    tomorrow i will decide the color of your shirt

and forget the difference between time and space
    for you will be in neither.

and still the rats feast in the orchard.

portrait of the woman at the bottom of the well

hollow tree filled full of bones where barn owls haunt thin as shadows /
smokesick from burning peat coughed up since turtle crawled out the swamp
with the world on his shell / dim stars too weak to reach the lake / all 'round
dead men wail / drowned walk on land 'til morning comes / coyote knows the
taste of man / an' church bells toll in funeral time / warn all who hear *be/ware
the/witch in/the well*

she old as glass / cloudy-eyed / long charcoal hair hangs loose in curls / lips taste
of nightshade / come full moon light coughs up lungs and heart / shakes loose
bloody stump of wings / aches for flight / pinions hang on churchyard steps /
steadied words read *for god so loved the world* / preacher teach to gathered mass
/ all cotton-eared and sealed with wax / to keep the honeyed songs away

mommas hold they babies close / when high winds howl in hurricane / say *she
snatch you up come dreamtime dark and eat you raw as oyster* / men say worse in
bars / bury stillborns in salt / watch daughters' backs for nubs of wings / carve
her out to keep them pure

found her trapped in iron rings / said she missed the rain / asked her why she
hates us so / told me the earth don't make mistakes so we're beauty to the bone /
and though god tells us we broken she loves us just because / and i had nothing
back to say so i left her there below / she cried straight through past evening-
time / still hear her sing / *will you be lonesome / when i'm gone*

the barbeque of the Taino prophet

remember tall Hatuey who,
when tied to a stake and given the choice
to convert and save his immortal soul,

asked whether heaven was full
of spaniards.

and when the priest said yes
he thought about it
for a minute
and finally said

he'd rather go to
hell
so he wouldn't have to spend
eternity
with such cruel folks.

so next time you question why
the south is full of
lonesome
ghosts

remember tall Hatuey
who burned alive and for his
trouble
now lives on as a
brand of

cigars,
to smolder on
'til the last sunset
crowns us like
the tongue of
god dipped in
bright
vermillion.

lovecraft was a city boy

green eyed dreams of broken things / black crow croak / i heard rats in the walls by the grapefruit trees 'til the night our liver-and-white bitch snarled through the kitchen / ground small bones to pulp / licked my face / 'cause she loved me so

words don't mean much when wasps crawl out of coke cans / half chewed / goddamn does coke dissolve shit fast / daddy says *check your boot yourself* / but you only kill the things you find / they only let you find 'em 'cause they ready to die / i know / 'cause jesus told me so outta the mud what dried where red bull gored two coyote / i hear their momma howl *come back to me my sons my sons come back*

moon don't care / that's all i got to say about that

sneak out the trailer when midnight comes / follow the ants / they know the way / pick 'em up by the scruff of their neck / shake loose their tiny tongues / i did it once and they told me *son we're off to see the king in yellow* / i knew enough about things to leave 'em be after that

see wingless white-eyed flies / come crawlin' to you cryin' *daddy daddy check my boots* / i got good news / when them growed-up maggots crawl through tattered sheets / they ain't real until you smoosh em / sweet dreams / i love you

David van den Berg

carcosa

i.
never found the lost city
cassilda sang lullabies in
dreams left me
frozen
from the chin up

ii.
bought a map at a thrift store
showed carcosa next to some sinkhole lake
black water shows truth upside down
dug straight through limestone rock
drained the whole swamp dry

iii.
my heart is a limestone slab
cassilda is the ocean
and will drain herself loving me

carcosa

found carcosa / buried / deep in clayhole pond / swamp down through mud / found clay tablets and the secrets / they kept / were / long erased / follow me in dreams / gold statues of tadpole kings / asked cassilda to love me / forever / and / ever / beneath two moons and a starlit sky / her silence is all / I can remember / 10 meters down / lungs / are half as big / if you breathe again / and swim back up / they burst like / fireflies / in swamp mist / air / what a sight / my mind moves / in circles and all that will / happen / has / happened / already / if you loved me / you could turn the moons back / to the time before / and pull the burs / off my soles / my heart / is a limestone slab / and / cassilda / is a /

hammer

David van den Berg

love letters from an arsonist

daddy was a wildfire burned hisself inside out / spat out pinecone sons what can only grow in flames / held me close so i burned his fingers / kissed me on flintlock mouth / belched smoke laughed *that's my boy*

i loved stars in tarry skies / pick 'em outta constellations like loose diamonds / turn to glass in greasy palms / smashed to pieces 'gainst chipped asphalt / said *walk on boy that bridge was made to burn / an' you more tindering than man*

drank gasoline from momma's breast / breathe fire when i dream / love you strong as devil winds / remember me when sky is red and night haze reads one hundred ten and moon is big as it's ever been / 'cause baby i've been burned before and you're the match for me

saw the future in the blaze / ash footprints walk backwards in half ghost steps / white corn liquor sings / an' all i ever was or am is nothin' like i hoped to be / found god out back makin' mash ask / why you make me like this / he say *there a hole deep down at the bottom of you* i ask why / he say / *'cause you're like me, my son.*

Grandma Voodoo's Motel Six

For the traveler seeking the *Authentik* South
the guidebook suggests staying the night (or two!)
at Grandma Voodoo's Motel Six,
just down the street from Liaf's Airboat Rides, the only place in town
that gae-run-tees at least two gator sightings and a real live Seminole
who'll wrestle lizards with turkey feathers in his hair (tips appreciated!)

The gang's all there for pictures, 10 to 2.
That's Brer Rabbit, Rawhead 'n Bones, and Tar Baby, with pillow paws and
    bobble heads.
At 6:15 sharp Grandma Voodoo comes out the kitchen to teach erryone how
    to bake
her deliciously evil love potion cupcakes (the secret ingredient is McCormick's
    cane sugar with frosted sprinkles).

For only 325 you can stay in a gen-u-ine replica of a Cracker shack,
and 50 more will let you wave a Confederate flag behind a souped up F-150
with a collectible white hood thrown in for 9.99 plus
roast s'mores on burning crosses for 2 bucks a pop
and you get a 10% discount on Thursday Cattle Rustling if you book online and
(unbelievable!)
children eat for free at the pinata lynching.

Now that's what I call Faulkner!

> [i met the real grandma voodoo once / in a hollow tree out past deadwood swamp
> fat and black as rich man's onyx / lips like sugarcane sandpaper tongue
> she pulled my soul out my bellybutton / stuffed it in a cat's eye shell
> and when i look in lakes i still have no reflection]

beloved

born chicken legs in rubber boots / two foot deep in wet concrete / preacher
called me son / of adam / held me / 'neath clear water 'til i saw fire / waitin' / at
world's end / 'cause the love of god is strong / as whiskey / and burns / like / lye

in new moon dreams Hyades shines / like pearls / at swamp bottom / filtered
through duckweed and / cigarette butts / stand thigh deep in quicksand / cas-
sandra washes me / in wet red / clay / says / the soul of the earth is / old / er
than the / dark / but / the stars are / dim / and / hungry / worlds will eat /
worlds / 'till all that's left is / hunger / calls me son / of atom / drowns me /
by the cypress knees / hollow eyed / 'cause the price of wisdom / is / madness

wake in damp sheets / mud / dy boots / train whistle blows two miles north /
like the wailing loon / night is full of / empty ghosts / and teeth / grow loose /
the eye / of taurus is / bluer / than before / sees all / i've done / lungs turn to /
stone / like how / granddad / went / and his dad before / run / towards daddy's
snores / climb in bed / by his belly / holds me / like i'm newly birthed / calls
me / just / beloved

David van den Berg

babe

ol' mr. lee had a wild hog trained to eat out his hand an' bathe in muddy orange groves an' the two cooed like mourning doves / pa scared it through barbed wire / i shot it dead with a .410 slug / lee saw / full grown man cried through scraggle beard / an' i never seen pa so shamed

i got regrets / biggest is i was gone when they took my pup an' pumped her full of sick / died empty so's all i got is a clay pawprint and the knowledge / that she shook 'till the end

now i'm four with a gun on my hip / pa says *squeeze that trigger* / down i go in sulfur smoke an' wake by warm whiskey with a knot like pine run through my gut / an' 20 years is a lifetime to some who bruise too easy / but the best parts of us last half that / 'cause the wages of sin is death an' too many coffins come size small / ask me how to stop it / all i got is / if my heart was a womb i'd sow it with salt and lye / so naught would grow but tumbleweeds

good luck charm

i got a brain like a alligator egg / wrinkled as leather an' white as snakeskin /
when it cracks *hoo boy* best watch out 'cause that thing is mad

only buy lotto tickets in threes / scratch silver paint with a buffalo nickel / a
pair means she loves me / empty pockets means she don't / locked in daisy
chains / 'til the horses hit the stretch / and racecards fall like / december rain

took a rabbit's foot offa some dead thing i found / all maggots and bad air an' /
tire tracks all over / rubbed that sucker on the flop / nothin' but aces and eights
/ told my red jacks they let me down / they said / *luck's not the measure of a man
/ but the love of god above / and boy / have we bad news for you*

gave my pennies to the witch in the well / told me / *no one ever loved you like
you needed* / well / that's showbiz baby and / i always bet on red

the witch-mama of nubbins slough

there's a woman deep down in okeechobee or nearbouts,
stands 4 foot 8 weighs three hunnerd pounds
balder'n a cue ball and got four whole teeth
between her top and bottom gums
and i ain't never loved a woman like her.

whole town knows she takes babies from girls
raises them on foxmilk.
some folks say at night they see a dark shape movin' slow
with a bald head slung over its shoulder bobbin'
here and there quiet like mornin' fog.
those who know better have never seen her and
say so 'til they face is blue.

saw preacher bury iron knives 'neath churchhouse steps
said *god don't want no part of Mama Black*
and drownt himself come new moon
with no teeth in his mouth and broken prayer
beads down his throat.

girls mama raise grow tall as oaks and laugh like fireflies
and don't stick around but go to big cities.
i hear they make the best damn surgeons you could find and
sleep with scalpels in they hand.

men pull catfish from mud with bare hands and
hunt racoons and possums and anything
they think mama might want.
buy her skin mags and tabloids
love her like a pup cooing with his eyes still shut
an' laugh at her big rubber kiss smacked fat on cheeks.

the secret to us is
men ain't nothin' but boys grown big
and look for mama 'til they put us in a pine box.

blood magic

i don't believe in ghosts / don't stop them haunting me / white flash hair raise
candle *whoosh* / lay 'neath sheets too thin for cold / count heartbeat some
distant drum / *badum badum* / birds don't call 'til 5 am / *badum badum* /
badum badum

pa taught me to bathe in blood / i got a gator's lungs / pig's heart / i could go on
/ swallowed mist 'til i forgot / where i stopped and it began

ain't nothin' special 'bout blood magic
earth's been drinkin' blood since time forgot / ain't helped much

if i got a pig's heart / who's got mine / lost myself in bits and pieces / all that's
left is stolen chunks what i sewed up with needle bone and spiderweb / what
kind of man it made / alone at 3 am while my woman sleeps / and i still walk
backwards outta darkened rooms

Ballad of Bull Creek

i.
my brother knew everything
and he told me about the monster who lived
beyond the barbed wire fence

ii.
not yet midnight
by the firing range
cattle call
coyote answers
don't go out that gate

iii.
rundown shed smells of gasoline and whiskey
inside
legless plastic turkeys
peppered with 12 gauge shot and
unlucky feathers
draw flies and flies
draw widows and widows
make love good enough to lose your head

iv.
if i were an animal i'd be a male black widow and i'd thank god for the opportunity

v.
monster lay beneath a palmetto bush
ribs gaunt glass eyes hot breath
gasping blueblack swamp air too weak
to shake the maggots free
we sat a while before
i brought myself to slit his throat
but i didn't know how thick it was
i sat with him 'til it was done
and cried the whole time

rise, Lazarus

in the valley of small shadows
my teeth   bloom
    like wild roses.

rot blossoms as   enamel
    peels   back
and my mouth fills with   sand so i can
    taste   pink froth
blood that leads   to
          nirvana.

in time the rains may come
    and wash the taste
of metal   from my dreams

but   until then
    may the backhoe
        open the earth
that the bodies we
    planted
might rise in   linen sheets,
    turn their chins
        up
and give   a mighty shout:
        Again! Again!

Herodotus Writes Concerning Eternal Life, 2019

Anyone with any sense knows that the Fountain of Youth is a hundred year old tourist trap outside St. Augustine. It is run by charlatans and their promises are as empty as the cottonmouth eggs they sell to boys.

Beware the billboards, tall and straight. The lies they tell are crooked as my spine now that I am an old man and full of spite.

There is no memory of the southern Calusa, who call themselves the Fierce People and believe that a man's three souls live in his pupil, his shadow, and his reflection. Who knows of the masked Senequne and his sister-wife? Who knows of the splendors of Calos? I say to you, the coward de León knows of their arrows bathed in the blood of the manchineel tree.

Woe to you who sow gar's teeth and pray for maize.

Here is the understanding of the magick of the Fountain, as explained by the greasy, pimpled attendant at the cash register: rich, elderly people enter stage right, carried by servants. Strip. Enter a pool. The people in the pool are young and beautiful and naked. After a while they exit stage left to attend a fabulous royal feast. Voila, youth.

Nonsense!

Such a transaction—exchanging death for life—is rooted deep in the magick of the Buzzard King and would never merely *envelop* a frail body, regardless of social status. A queen ant is still an ant, and the Buzzard King lives in a nest 30 miles high (it is known).

Here is the truth.

An ancient shrine is hidden south of the phosphate mines in Bone Valley (here I am relying on the testimony of a Spaniard I encountered while fishing who claimed to be two hundred and eighty years old). The entrance, he said, is nestled in a burrow guarded by a mighty alligator close to 20 feet long. You must offer her a live goat and if she eats it whole you are permitted to crawl between her petrified eggs and into the hollow beneath.

The way is lit by luminescent moss. You will see a mighty cypress tree that is fed by a dark green stream. Do not touch the water, for it will turn you to copper. Clamber over cypress knees to reach the tree itself which you will find covered in purple flowers that attract ants and bees in copious amounts. The insects gorge themselves on the nectar and are sweet to the taste.

(Perhaps you say that this seems strange, but I remind you that I have been to the Nile and I have seen horses with necks close to 10 feet long and small, harmless serpents with horns on their head and I have seen the Earth open up and swallow a mansion whole and stranger sights still).

Once every two hundred years, the cypress tree blooms: a ruby red fruit at the very top of the tree. When it is ripe all animals within 5 leagues go mad. The crowd of men (women are forbidden by the oracles of the Buzzard King) who have gathered in the burrow then set upon each other as beasts, snarling and convulsing to the hisses of waiting vultures *long live the king*.

When one man remains he climbs the tree and eats the fruit, described as having the taste of the tangerine and the consistency of the coconut. He is granted a lifetime for each man he slew in the hollow, and the buzzards and the cypress tree feast on the dead for years to come.

So sayeth the Buzzard King:
eat up!

The Palace of the Rhinoceros

i. *The Promenade*

people stream like army ants
off the loose packed dirt road that leads to
pensacola

beat up jeeps and sleeper vans blare punk
and dime store rap and cough black soot
on topless husks of
men built of twigs and and bleach

ii. *The High Gate*

stairs creak
porch rot
two pumpkins stomped, one filled with glass
and bloody footprints two by two
no door to keep the snows away

iii. *The Antechamber*

women lie on beds made from orange juice bottles and tin empties
watched by ten thousand eyes on walls more graffiti than wood

no floor but torn clothing and old magazines and mcdonalds bags
stacked three feet high and stinking like dirty coins

iv. The Throne Room

atop his golden throne sits the Rhino King
glass eyes red with see through skin
poachers took his horn left bulging veins and cracked lips
and he laughs and he laughs and he laughs and he laughs

everything you think happens here
happens here

and if i didn't know myself better
i might even go with cash in my pocket

the one thing we all know is
the dreams you dream by the Rhino King
always come true

i dreamt my generation was a mighty forest
felled in a single stroke

Epistle II:

The Midnight Gospel

midnight gospel

listen.

mudcats sing of the upside-down where the damned fry in cast-iron. pa taught me to dry chicken livers and slip 'em onto hooks, and said we had do-minion over the creeping things of the land and the things of the sea and the things of the sky, and when brother winged a doe we called her tripod and every three-legged white tail we crossed was forever spared.

quail tell that the sun is naught but the barrel of a 20 gauge, and the righteous spend their lives in the dirt but the vainglorious cross its face in flight just to fall in thunder. ma taught me to train the dogs with iron hand and when the doctor fed my black-and-white bitch poison she called to say the soul was eternal and the dark beyond is filled with love, and whether we're in heaven or hell depends on if you'll take it.

but the owl told me he's not scared of nothing 'cause his big eyes saw that our spirit lives in our shadow and grows longer with each hurt we cause 'till that shadow is big as a peacock's tail, and when we die it weighs us down so we struggle to take flight, and spend the rest of time creepin' underfoot until the things that have do-minion over us wake from their long sleep and swallow us whole. and i'd doubt him but i know better since seeing the veil in a mirror at the wake of april last.

the book of lamentations

weep, Jerusalem.

i fear the dry beat of chains less than the voice of my Jesus howlin' through the
    eyewall that
the LORD has come to take my first born to the bottom of the river,
makes me stay up 'til dawn falls like red dot yolk in cast iron,
an' though it's a long way to heaven it's six feet down to forever.

the LORD is a map and the law is a maze and folks confuse the difference.

the land of my fathers is choked with chalk bones lost to ghosts who know
    nothin' but sweat an' leather
where dusk sees cypress heads bloom strange dark fruits that
smell of kerosene and raw iron.
and daddy's jaws flash white, sayin' *we are the body eaters*
while i wait for the LORD to send
the flood that was promised.

i hear His voice in the space left in throats where last gasps rise like red suns
    at midnight,
says He does not bring punishment but
payment.

Jerusalem!
we carry the sins of our fathers; must we now weigh down our sons?
Jerusalem!
the river rises; will you deny the fever beneath?
Jerusalem!
your past is writ in blood; would you pluck out your eye to spite your brother?

David van den Berg

while my woman slept my Jesus came to me and promised
the end of all
first in fire
then
in
darkness.

ontological odontology

teeth are the seeds of the soul. incisors for the curious, cuspids for the proud, molars for the fatalists. sow them as Jason, see what springs forth.

rodents lack canines, relying on curved incisors set deep in jaws that grow until death. the tusks of the wise elephant are enlarged incisors providing tactile exploration, whereas the tusks of the deer-pig babirusa are enlarged canines and, if left to grow unchecked, will pierce the babirusa's own skull. baboons have enlarged canines for defense and display, such as against the self-sharpening carnassials of the matriarchal spotted hyena, who are born with their eyes open and whose premolars can outbite a grizzly and allow the hyena to eat its prey bones and all. the crushed bone colors the hyena's scat white: woe to you who seek the laughing beast. strange is the proteroglyphous black mamba with hollow fangs that lay flat until the serpent bites, flooding its victim with venom. stranger still are those hollow-toothed cobras who spit venom in geometric patterns and who in turn are bested by the flat topped molars of large monitor lizards, which will grind all things to dust.

the human mouth has been mapped, adapted, imprisoned, resculpted, and otherwise made redundant. we have no soul hiding in our pearly whites. here is the rub:

through history, many have sworn they have seen god's face.

but have they seen his teeth.

what violent delights wait for us behind his tightened lips.

when the last days come, our end will not be prophesied by war and famine and plague,

but by a grin.

Prosperity Gospel Blues

remember the miracle of loaves and fishes when the crowds went hungry and he walked away with five thousand in the bank? walked all the way across the lake in italian leather penny loafers the color of a warm cognac. said *god's a man of taste* and joined the money lenders of the temple in the bull market of salvation. i'd buy and sell souls too but my credit's shot and the bank won't accept fisher of man as a source of income. still it feels good to worship God-in-the-Three-Piece-Suit on sundays when the rabbit ears pick up local public access broadcasts and preacher comes into the trailer with his teeth white as the lamb he eats to say that i can be rich like him if i give now. and though heaven's limited to platinum-level donations i can still get a rent-to-own mobile home in spitting distance of st. pete. i told Cass all about it when she closed me out and she said that preacher stank of moral bankruptcy and gin. all i could think was if God didn't want him to be rich then why'd He make him so damn handsome?

the ghost of all things

it's best to speak of god in darkened rooms / 'cause the old man's cataracts are thick as silver dollars / ears sharp and cold as shattered glass / hears our endless whispers like / 3am static of a black-and-white tv / can't sleep so / he's meaner than a hornet / stalks the heavens with week-old stubble / hollow cheeked / lookin' for some sucker to smite just 'cause he can.

he'd love us more but / he loved the first of us too much / couldn't bear to lose 'em to the night beyond the stars so / he caught hold of the pain and the grief and the other heavy things they left behind / ordered it to pass from father to son and mother to daughter so / he'd never have to say goodbye.

but it weighs too much / never measured up to memory / now when he looks at us he sees naught but / coulda-beens and empty hopes / and while we live we pass that disappointment down the road. / and the ghost of all things lives inside our bones and we blame ourselves for who we are but / i don't look kindly on the man who'll place a curse on seven generations / or the one who'll use our wings to teach us how to drown.

on finding another mass grave at a residential school

outrage comes easy like a bull on red. still hollow as snaketooth,
leaves me asking what good them deaths did, 'cause *martyr* is another word
for *we had things too good to bother changing.*

in the city of weeping children, angels live as pigeons on gray buildings
and report that people are kind because
the dumpsters fill with bread.

David van den Berg

a history of the antediluvian times

when god made man he took one of those fat-bottomed fertility statues and filled it with an electrical fire, but was surprised to find that we grew teeth, and when he tired of the shocks we gave he sent the flood to melt us down. but he's a lousy engineer (if you can't tell by the full beds in the NICU) so's all he did was spread the flames 'till he threw up his hands and swore good and loud that that was that and took all his toys to go home like a spoiled child, and left us hungry 'cause our nature is to burn. so when the good book tells you that when the end of days comes we will perish in flames, don't believe it, 'cause fire is the heart of you and the world looks mighty dry to me.

i dreamed god was an astronaut

and never asked why comets smelled like moonshine.

somewhere is a network of men who don't know how deep lonely goes.
together they bounce messages off shooting stars in search of answers
to questions they can't ask sober.

satellites hear prayers but somewhere between reception and transmission
drop the call. perhaps evil
is naught but
indifference
to suffering.

i have questions
for the angels of the thermosphere. like is it true they take bets
on which hurricane will hit hardest? what is the spread and
which bank will cash them out? am i still bad from 60 miles up
or does it all make sense up there?
can i be seen at all?

hubble found god in the eagle nebula. took a picture
of the absent rocketeer with his feet up on a red dwarf
like he owned the place.

folks rushed to radio pleas his way but
that'll just piss him off
if the signals block the game.
doesn't matter.
a picture's just the past and he'll be long gone
before their prayers arrive
as only fathers can.

2 cent prophet

jeremiah was a boy when god touched him on the mouth
and muhammad hid in caves when the angel came for him
and jesus allowed himself to die for everybody's sins
but when god called me at 3 am he sounded low and beat
asked if i should write it down he said *it just won't help,*
they don't read with soul no more and i'm tired anyhow
so i asked him for a line, some final epilogue
he said *i guess just say,* then sighed and paused real long,

good luck, everyone.

james 5: 1-6

hear me
though you have stuffed your
    e a r s with
           precious silks
to drown the beating of another's h e a r t.

weep!
howl!
the miseries that shall soon befall you are
          beyond counting.

i have seen the
     n i g h t s
        that are to come and
i have seen your
     w e a l t h
        turn to ash and
i have seen your
     f i n e t h i n g s
        scattered in branches of dead pines
where moths and worms
     have made a home
        of your memory.

your gold and silver will c a n k e r and
you will c l u t c h at them as drowning men and
they shall e a t your flesh like fire
to forever b r a n d your soul
as
wanting.

you have heaped upon yourself treasures in the time of burning.

you have declared the fruits of your brother far sweeter and have left your
sister
to lie hungry in the street,

and when she asked for bread for her mewling kits
you asked why they could not feed on water.

you have fatted yourself in the days of slaughter. do you doubt the butcher's
hand?

the day of judgment lies in the hands of those
whose h e a r t s you have eaten and
who you let live u n b u r i e d as walking dead and
who you buried u n m a r k e d in common ground so that
your s h a m e is hidden from your sight.

am i now your enemy for bringing you the truth?
rejoice, for the word of god is b i t t e r and
the world has chosen
d e a f n e s s.

between me and the mangrove tree

a secret.

i first met god in the pisser of a run down club way out beyond the lights of
    old town
where he stiffed the blind black bathroom attendant who called him *sir* and
    offered him sprays of
cheap cologne and stale peppermints.

when i found my words i asked him what he thought
of my poems. told me
i wrote about ghosts too much.

i said it was his fault
for puttin' them there.

but he told me ghosts aren't as lonely as i thought 'cause
they go right back to the start like a needle on vinyl
drops back through the river of melody
to the same white whine of nothing.
get a chance to do it all over just the same.

told him i thought that was worse and he
just stared at me like he never thought of that
before settling in with a beer, saying
that was just a matter of opinion.

David van den Berg

now am i become death

always afeared of that long night / as a tadpole i lay 'neath the bed between the spare mattress and wall / prayed to three saints i knew and one / i made up / wasn't ready when they answered back / told me / hell's gates flash neon / VACANCY / like them hotels where men rent rooms by the hour and women wear high heels 'til dawn / 'cause the devil don't want us to feel too outta place

i press 'em on heaven / where the gates is shut and angels tattoo prayers 'cross throats / and graffiti reads like lightning / cracklin' sharp and cold since / god turned off the heat and locked hisself away 'cause the critics wrote / *the universe is not your best work* / and his children only learned the worst of him

i told 'em to give me wisdom / or a sign / or wonders / so i could preach the midnight gospel / they said n*o one listens anyhow / and besides / you already know where you goin'.*

David van den Berg

like the last few drops of rain

birds weren't made to fly
but learned anyway and now
no one imagines otherwise.

    (so too your bones,
    hollow,
    'neath fevered skin
    weren't made to carry those things
    the world would not let you
    leave behind.)

tell me why the mockingbird sings
in the witching hour
when the owls are on the hunt?

did they hear what is to come
when the beyond is far behind?

does the curtain shut to wild cheers or
do the lights just
go
out?

listen.

the one perched by the window sings that it is as the end of a storm
the last few drops of rain
then cometh the calm.

(there is no birdsong full enough
to quiet the empty echoes
in those places you last laughed.

but know
the one-eyed mockingbird you loved
still waits on the red gum tree
and when he sees me
whistles the tune you taught.)

prayer for peace

last time i saw god at the dive bar on 50
he fished for some small talk while the
bartender poured his double scotch neat.
settled on askin' if we had figured out
how to live in peace yet. i said *no not quite.*
and he asked if we had tried killin' other
peoples' kids and i said *yeah we're pretty
good at that.* then the bartender pushed the
scotch over and as the old man walked off
he said maybe if we kept it up we'd figure
things out.

gethsemane

thank you for the cold 'cause i'm grateful for the sunlight. thank you for the hunger 'cause i'm grateful for the rain. thank you for yesterday 'cause i'm grateful for tomorrow. thank you for the broken bone 'cause i'm grateful just to dance. thank you for the fire 'cause i'm grateful for what's left. maybe you ain't heard but things are bad down here. the garden is in drought and california smells like smoke. i ain't heard much from you but i'm waiting just the same, and it's not in the Book but here's the last thing jesus said: *are you sure about this* and, hand to heart, here's what God said back:

i'm going to hell (and who cares!)

listen
to the gospel i bring.

the good news is:
i'm going to hell.

who cares!

i got my sword in my hand
i leeched and scrounged
        (hallelujah!)

drank more whiskey than twain
stole not 'cause i needed to but
'cause i could
and worst of all

i made my momma cry

tight clear dewdrops as she said
what did i do
to make someone like you?

and i'm sayin this but
i ain't confessing and i do
not
repent.
i will live with lead in my heart and
pray for misery and sickness until the day
the devil puts me on a train and i pull into that fiery station and
he bellows out

63

welcome home brother
we missed you somethin' strong

but i'm okay with that.

cause i know who's goin' to heaven.
an' you know who i mean.
we know because they told us so.

here's what jesus say.
jesus say
when i was hungry you didn't give me any meat.
when i was nekked you wouldn't give me no clothes.
i was in prison and you didn't come for me.
i fled war and you sent me home to die in rubble and
ruin.

so thank god po-lice lock up the homeless
and millionaire preachers yell to
build walls to keep those refugees out.
i'd hate to come face to face with that man
just for him to tell me he loves me anyway.

and i think i feel like that
because

loving someone
truly. deeply.
is to see the rotted wood inside their heart
and love them even more

and
i'll be honest

i don't think my heart was made for loving

but every night i dream i'm wrong.

babel

maybe the bees were right / when god gave 'em their choice of / tongues / and they said / *no thanks* / *we'll dance instead* / 'cause what can that / thin / muscle / say / to fill the / space / between here and / gone?

the holler / has a / tongue / all its own / drowned in saltpeter an' / rust / spoke by / haints / an' grieving mothers huddled / on dark bundles / in blue lights of midnight. / an' where / greek / mariners / fixed their ears with / cotton / to skirt / temptation / folks now / stitch the lips of the / dead / so ghosts / cannot cry for / judgement.

before god was the word / before babel the flood / before you was mem'ry / before me the dark.

Epistle III:

Pinecone Son

pinecone son

i am a shadow dreamt he was the moon.

this is the way of things:

the last time a star sets you will feel an empty well open and not know why.
i let waves wash over me to know what it means to feel lightness
and if i squeeze my eyes tight i can pretend that i am under a thick blanket
and the weight of the ocean comes warm and calm like yesterday's sun.

tonight i will call my mother to say that i will not be home for christmas
but better days are coming.

somewhere between the mountain and the valley
lies salvation. i hear the garden is well stocked and
the epilogue is worth finishing the book.

the season of sleeplessness will come.
on the nights you lie awake as your breath catches hard in your ribs
and your heart beats hollow through your throat,
look to the bottom of an ink-black cloud.
i will be watching and
together
we will wait for dawn.

woodman and coldwater

she fell into me with her life bundled in two
hefty-brand trashbags
and sat for a while and
when i asked where she wanted to go, she closed her eyes and asked me to take her to
some canyon
somewhere.

instead of an address she dropped a pin in the wilderness and i said *are you sure*
and she said it didn't matter
much
so long as i got her out of the city.

i took the 101 west,
past strip malls and 24 hour donut shops and the browning astroturf of the putt putt
park and the million little ghosts that live in wreckage we leave behind.

the setting sun filled her lungs with glass so
her breaths came raw and ragged and
i watched her through the rearview mirror.
she fought back sleep as her phone rang and rang and each time she hung up a little
bit slower.
just a little bit slower.

and i said *we're supposed to get rain this weekend, that should be nice* and waited for
nothing and she put her phone down and so i said i *miss it, you know. makes me think
    of home* and
together
we stared into the dark of what lay before us,
illuminated by the endless glow of brakelights.
she was beautiful, i guess.
but didn't look it.
she wore sickness like a cloak. all hollow eyes and emptiness,
sweating and shaking beneath a jacket that she pulled close around her bones.

the only thing keeping her awake was the wasp that lived inside her phone.
buzzing and biting and buzzing and stinging
as though the world would end if it fell silent.

then
with tires screaming and horn bleating this
motherfucker
ran me off the road and i slammed on the brakes and her bags ripped open
    and out came a waterfall of
empty orange bottles and dirty clothes and other things that used to
mean something.

and i said *shit* and she said *i'm sorry* and i said *nah* but she didn't let me talk,
just kept saying
i'm sorry i'm sorry i'm sorry.
i grabbed the tiny bottles and saw the labels.

goodbye notes
in pharmacy script.
unread.

i offered them to her but she
held what was left of her world in her arms and collapsed inside herself until
she almost drowned and she
whispered
can i change
where i'm going.

and i nodded.

and she sighed a deep, deep sigh. wiped her nose and
asked
me to take her to the hospital.

when i dropped her off i called my mom and
told her that

i

loved
her.

be gentle to each other.
the world is too small for our hearts and
there are too many notes left

unread.

David van den Berg

migratory patterns of the lonely heart

wrote a love note on the side of a freight train signed in
cigarette ash and montana black.
if you love her, let her fly north
with the shrikes and the thunder of the
union pacific
before all things fall to embers,
and i scoop up scattered carbon so my fingers taste of
burnt marshmallow and turpentine,
and here i stand before a boxcar as i tell you
physics
lets time move forwards or back, so
in a way
i never let you go,
and in a way
you're home again,
and in a way,
i never missed you
much
at all.

David van den Berg

psalm 51

look
if i could shed
    skins
as well as the next i'd be scrubbed
        pink
like a jackdaw fresh popped
    and
halfway to tahiti

    but

my spine of spines
    rises
from the sea, wine-
        dark
where i live one
    breath
to the next like an echo of
        some memory
as my lungs,
            pink and raw,
fill like bellows in tune to flashes—
        slow-crawl satellites at dusk—
and i whisper to
    the floorboards
i exist i exist i exist i exist
        as though
that was all it took.

Misha forgive me
        on the banks of the
                        Blackwater
where i held you
            under
murky water's thick hued sheen—
                        kicking—
for a handful of
        gold-
capped teeth found deep in the
                belly
of a bullhead.

                    look! look!
the sun
            has forgotten
to rise and in its absence
                    i may find
absolution.

David van den Berg

song for the drowning

deaf say they thought the sun made noise
and were sad to hear nothing much at all
come dawn
'cause silence is a gift for those
who don't know how good they got it.

music plays slow underwater
where even drowning looks like dancing
and treble leaves bass at surface 'till all that's left
is violins
and if you stay deep enough with shrunken lungs
you could half believe you're flying.

love in lead boots.
the ocean is deeper than the grave and
i fear drowning less than being alone.

the best little strip club in florida

caught dead in a too well lit college bar when
i turned and said
fuck this
where's trouble

sped east
whooped and sang for 40 miles
parked to piss on a stop sign and looked for road beers through the darkened
    windows of a sunoco
then 20 more and found ourselves
by the blacked out doors of a beachside titty bar

the owner looked us over
    (we're young and strong and will never ever die)
whistled and said

man
the girls are gonna
love
you

first thing i saw was
a man wrapped around some girl
    (like the flapping canvas of an unmoored tent)
head in her shoulder, eyes closed,
fingertips white and desperate for
someone to hold on
to.

anyone.

and women walked by with
beer bellies hanging over g-strings and
they shook lopsided tits and somehow had
one whole ass between them

and one sat on my lap and told me
i could buy her and a hotel room for

practically nothing

and a divorce lawyer handed me a stack of ones
and his business card
and told me the girl on stage looked lonely

and one who kept forgetting her stage name told me
my eyes were too sad for my face and
don't i know she could fix that

and when i said i wouldn't buy a dance from one she said
she must not be my type because
she knew she was the
most beautiful
girl in the place
      (well she wasn't)
      (and she wasn't)

and all the while that man sat
holding on as tight as he could
because if he let go
the ocean would take him and
never
      (ever)
spit
him
out.

David van den Berg

bacchus is a barren god

i pray best on quarter beer night

burnt out bathroom bulbs give a holy glow to vague outlines of men

we all speak the same language:
beer and disappointment

curse
bodies that failed us and
women who left us
and those goddamn
shanked cue balls

and if i get good and drunk
i can't help but look for something beautiful in that cracked bathroom mirror

but all i find is me

stoneheart

would you miss my stone
            heart
if i peeled its yellow wallpaper
        back
like the dried sap of the gum tree you hate?

the air is cold and the bed is w i d e and
the sheets were last
            washed
when i said what i said (and what i said was the truth)
    ((which i guess made it worse))
like how a star will go dark
            and no one will know
like how our sun will go dark
            and no one will know.

so will you miss my stoneheart at
                    night
'cause i'm afraid to go dark like the
sun in the sky
            and no one will know.
you can write on my stone the truth of it all:
if you were worth missing
you wouldn't have left.

i'm afraid to write love poems

i drove up the angel's highway the night i went to watch the sky fall

passing
abandoned cars and camper vans and parked a ways
away
from the clinking glasses and champagne laugh bubbling from
the tinted windows of a bmw.

i stood on the edge of the canyon
turned my eyes to the lion and let the bitter wind
eat me alive.

but
i saw no stars in the thinning air.
just a fat moon burnt orange by the western blaze
and
clouds of smoke built from
dreams
of men and women asleep in
parking lots.

and beneath my wings i saw
the city lights struggling to breathe to the rhythm of the
thunder of thousands of distant freeway trucks, so many and so faint that i thought
the ocean lived between their wheels.

i think
the second most beautiful thing i saw up there was the
ghost of a hanging tree
growing out of a boulder that cracked beneath its own weight.

the most beautiful thing i saw on the angel's highway,
of course,
was

you.

David van den Berg

Rose Petal Bandits (by Mr. Toad)

fox eyes bright in flashing sun
(you the fox and me the toad
 and try to tell me different)

fox says
thorns are made for scritching
white rose bad
and red rose good
run away mr. toad, eagles ho!

newspaper says
today the president did something bad
and soldiers shot their guns
and many people are very angry
and they should be!
(again! again!)

fox says
spring is when we make it

so why not steal roses from the churchyard bush?
and lavender from the cemetery?
happiness borrowed is not happiness stolen.

mr. toad has seen enough of mud

fox says
the air is filled with honeysuckle dreams
but you have to breathe it first.

never trust a dog who only loves you at dinner

cigarettes and dollar store perfume.
pupils big as dimes and
the iron of a thousand rusted fish hooks.

we left with the low tide and he slapped that wheel and said

> *i don't know how i do it but*
> *i make 'em fall in love with me.*
> *just like*
> *that*
> *they're in love.*

he grinned
(like a yella dog in mud)
and said

> *i'm bad. so bad.*

west we went and
i felt the line tighten and the hooks
tore through my skin until the blood flowed clear
but
i didn't say nothin' 'cause
i know his soul got more leaks than mine.

he just slapped that leather wheel of his
trashed his empty wallet
wiped purple lipstick off his nose and muttered
more to himself than me

just like that.
they're in
love.

i dunno. maybe they are.

and if they're not, who cares?

i mistook sabotage for humility

the secret is
if you believe you don't deserve love then,

in time,

everyone around you
will see that you
were right

from the start.

dear icarus

i found a polaroid of you and me at thirteen and you
wore a tie and held a balloon and i had some top hat on with glasses and we both
looked so serious that i—
well, anyway.

did you always know that you would fly?
even there in the hallway when you sold pecker pills to the other kids and i said
shit i'll take one and you said *nah it's only sudafed*
even when half-naked, you and i ran laughing through pale old english tourists
'cause i remember the last time i saw what you became as you
cried
and tried to wash your face out of the mirror.

icarus, i'm sorry.
i saw the scars but
didn't ask where your feathers had gone.

and i have so many questions now
and you aren't here to answer them.
just know that i can see you then
alone and
scared and losing
blood
and
icarus
when you stepped off that balcony
did you look back at all?

Fly United

i was 30,000 feet up when the pilot said the Cavs had won and i didn't give
two shits but this old man behind me from the ivory coast dressed in a suit
and tie jumped up and started dancing

and the flight attendants all laughed and even the hard hearted amongst us
smiled because it was so pure and real and warm and he hugged us all and sat
back down and i just wondered

what is that like?

to be so filled with joy and peace
that he would dance and sing aboard a plane
and he shook my shoulder and said
my brother today god loves you too

and if you have that light in you, i ask you now
share it just a little more often
for those like me who live in darkness
and spend our lives without

David van den Berg

of things that burn

i'm not made of flesh and bone
but candle wax.

tell me,

does the wick not fear the match?

and when the burning season comes
is not darkness a relief?

mithras rising

feather in a cyclone, tumbledry weeds.

he stumbled out the door at 2 am
watched the moon set in the rearview mirror and
headed for the highway.

a cop car was poorly hidden behind a tree by the westbound ramp so
he blinked hard and
drove east
towards the atlantic
to see the sun rise.

radio turned to static and
he sang what few words he could remember
from
whatever songs he heard that night.
turned on the air—as cold and high as it could go—and
passed the plastic golf course carved from the forest for those who
love the natural beauty of florida's par threes.
eyes itched and he rubbed first one
then the other
shut them
for just
a
second

when

he woke on the beach.

a crab nipped his toes to see if he was good for eating but
he flinched and it
scurried sideways down a tunnel until all that was left of it
was a single eyestalk and an angry claw that waved from the sand.
and he rolled over on his back and tasted
fresh rain
lightly falling from a cloudless sky.
the wind brought the cool ocean air and the sun
looked at him so friendly and
the sand was so soft
and
it all was
so
beautiful.

his pants were folded neatly nearby.
smelled of
piss
and
handsoap.
as he put them on a
note fell from a leg and he picked it up and saw the watery remnants of
someone else's handwriting,
the careful loops and solid lines washed away.
next to the pants he found a full bottle of water and an unopened pack of
crackers and on the bottle were three words, written in sharpie:
love yourself more.

and he sat on the beach
and ate the crackers
and fed seagulls
and found a periwinkle
and asked the crab

where does the magic go?

where did the magic go

and he missed his home.

very much.

then it was time

so he found his car double parked in the public lot. drove west. past things he
didn't remember passing in the night.
walked back in his apartment.
empty. cold.
no one there to worry where he'd been or
hear about the crab he met that day or
the kindness he'd found in ruined notes.

so he turned on the tv, the radio, the computer.
turned the volume up as loud as he could.
and went to bed.

David van den Berg

that's all, folks

i reckon that's it, friends. pa promised he'd never lie to me and proved it when i got the text that said it's cancer in the leg and i should come home quick. but people don't look like the deer that lay bleeding, eyes wide like it heard some shocking secret about the end. people look small wrapped in blankets with skin hanging like loose toilet paper over tree branches, eyes taped shut like windows at midwinter. the only thing same is their tongues seem too big for their mouths. keeps them from spillin' secrets.

i think it was noble of him to keep that promise and i make it to you too: the things you read are true or true enough, or the truth in sunday clothes. i think i did well enough. tell that to st. peter.

there's dignity in suffering and i suffered enough, but not as much as you. i hope you read me with charity and i hope you love you more than i love me, and i hope you have someone you can lean over and say *hey i love you* to and i hope that if you don't you're all the better for it.

and next time someone gives you good news i want you to say the last words granddaddy told me, with a fat smile on his face:

bullshit!

Acknowledgments

My undying thanks to my wife, who was forced to hear each poem multiple times. If reading this collection has infuriated you, spare a moment to pity her.

My thanks to my family, who tolerated each "Acceptance!" message to the group chat. If you believe it, my parents even put some of their favorite poems on a tackboard in the kitchen. Sure, it's not refrigerator-level praise, but it's pretty damn close.

Finally, I am so grateful for Lance Ümmenhofer and the rest of the April Gloaming staff. Their literary journal published some of my earliest writing, and their commitment to amplifying the voices of the unbridled holler is nothing short of incredible. I am so fortunate to be included in their publication lineup, and I urge you to check out the other great books they've put out.

Additional thanks to the following journals that published my poems previously: *Saw Palm, Rappahannock Review, Poetry South, Yemassee, South 85 Journal, Waxing & Waning, The American Journal of Poetry, From Whispers to Roars, The Ilanot Review, The Blue Mountain Review, Reality Break Press, Cathexis Northwest Press, Forbidden Peak Press,* and *Castabout Art and Literature.*

About the Author

David van den Berg grew up hunting and fishing in the Florida swamps. He studied anthropology, religion, and archaeology at Rollins College before moving to Los Angeles to work as an actor and to fulfill his life's dream of chauffeuring angry strangers. That adventure ended with a J.D. and a Master of Laws in Taxation from Loyola Law School. He is the founder of *Prometheus Dreaming* (@promethesudreamingmag), a digital literary journal. His poetry has recently appeared in *Saw Palm, Rappahannock Review, Yemasse, South85, Poetry South, The Ilanot Review, The American Journal of Poetry, Waxing & Waning,* and elsewhere. His chapbook, *Love Letters from an Arsonist,* was a finalist in the 2020 Kallisto Gaia Press Contemporary Chapbook Competition. His poem "the ghost of all things" was nominated for the 2021 Best of the Net prize. You can find him on Instagram @ohnonotthatguygoddamnit. And if you read this far, thank you.

About the Author

CPSIA information can be obtained
at www.ICGtesting.com
Printed in the USA
LVHW092349070423
743341LV00035B/433